GROUNDHOG
GETS A SAY

To Charlotte, my guardian groundhog,

and to underrated animals everywhere

—P.C.S.

For Buzz and the Crows—my guides and inspiration

—D.B.

Special thanks to Kathy Dawson, an editor who likes rodents;

to Freda Remmers, a wildlife rehabilitator who rescues them;

to Denise Brunkus, who draws them like no one else;

and to Bill Moody, who lets them share his vegetables.

PUFFIN BOOKS
Published by the Penguin Group
Penguin Young Readers Group, 345 Hudson Street, New York, New York 10014, U.S.A.
Penguin Group (Canada), 90 Eglinton Avenue East, Suite 700, Toronto, Ontario, Canada M4P 2Y3
(a division of Pearson Penguin Canada Inc.)
Penguin Books Ltd, 80 Strand, London WC2R ORL, England
Penguin Ireland, 25 St Stephen's Green, Dublin 2, Ireland (a division of Penguin Books Ltd)
Penguin Group (Australia), 250 Camberwell Road, Camberwell, Victoria 3124, Australia
(a division of Pearson Australia Group Pty Ltd)
Penguin Books India Pvt Ltd, 11 Community Centre, Panchsheel Park, New Delhi - 110 017, India
Penguin Group (NZ), 67 Apollo Drive, Rosedale, North Shore 0745, Auckland, New Zealand
(a division of Pearson New Zealand Ltd)
Penguin Books (South Africa) (Pty) Ltd, 24 Sturdee Avenue, Rosebank, Johannesburg 2196, South Africa

Registered Offices: Penguin Books Ltd, 80 Strand, London WC2R ORL, England

First published in the United States of America by G. P. Putnam's Sons, a division of Penguin Young Readers Group, 2005
Published by Puffin Books, a division of Penguin Young Readers Group, 2007

5 7 9 10 8 6 4

Text copyright © Pamela Curtis Swallow, 2005
Illustrations copyright © Denise Brunkus, 2005
All rights reserved

THE LIBRARY OF CONGRESS HAS CATALOGED THE G. P. PUTNAM'S SONS EDITION AS FOLLOWS:
Swallow, Pamela Curtis.
Groundhog gets a say / by Pamela Swallow; illustrated by Denise Brunkus.
p. cm.
Summary: Two groundhogs describe their various characteristics to a skeptical squirrel and crow.
Text includes various facts about groundhogs.
ISBN: 0-399-23876-X (hc)
[1. Woodchuck—Fiction. 2. Squirrels—Fiction. 3. Crows—Fiction.]
I. Brunkus, Denise, ill. II. Title.
PZ7.S969895Gr 2005 [E]—dc22 2004027545

Puffin Books ISBN 978-0-14-240896-4

Manufactured in China

Designed by Gina DiMassi.
Text set in Fontoon.
The art was done in watercolor and colored pencil.

FEBRUAR
2

GROUNDHOG
GETS A SAY

As told to
Pamela
Curtis Swallow

Illustrated by

Denise Brunkus

FEBRUARY

3

PUFFIN BOOKS

I don't get it. Where is everybody? Yesterday I was BIG news, a star, king of the mound! Everyone wanted my weather report. Today . . . nothing! This happens every year. My holiday ought to last longer than a day! I don't just do weather. Groundhogs deserve better! A week maybe. No, make that a month. February should be Groundhog Appreciation Month."

"You think I'm just a groundhog?
Nope. I'm also called a whistle pig.
In danger, I whistle VERY loud. And then I go . . .
Phew!—as in Phew, it's over. Danger past."

"He's trying to make us think that name's all about the whistle and not about his piggyness."

"I can think of a few other names to call him. Like Mr. Full of Himself."

"Hey, you're talking about my hero."

"And I've even got a third name—woodchuck.
If only I had a dollar for every time someone asked me,
'How much wood would a woodchuck chuck
if a woodchuck could chuck wood?'
The truth is—I'm not into chucking wood.
I'm more interested in moving dirt . . .
LOTS of it."

"Maybe the poem should go,
'How much ground could
a groundhog hog . . .'"

"I'm a digging machine. I can move about seven hundred pounds of dirt and rocks in one day. And how about this— my ears don't even get dirty! I have ear flaps to keep them clean."

"Yeah, but look at the rest of you."

"Actually, groundhogs clean up nicely. We're very neat."

"I don't dig any old which-way. First I go down a few feet and then up a foot, and then down again. That hump is my flood bump—it keeps the burrow from getting soaked in a storm. See, groundhogs are always thinking.

"My burrow's popular. Neighbors scoot in to avoid danger. Some can't wait to move in when I move out."

"You can pick your friends, but not your family."

"People everywhere love groundhogs.
We're in the family of rodents called marmots,
so the people who love us are called marmotophiles.
Folks who study us are called marmoteers!
Or marmotologists!"

"Not groundhogologists?"

"Or people with too much time?"

"I can think of a few folks who aren't fans of your so-called cousin over there."

"Right. Remember the mess he made of Mr. Moody's garden?"

"Gardeners can be very excitable."

"You think I have to stay on the ground?
Only if I want to.
I can climb trees."

"So now he's a treehog too.
But let's see him fly."

"Or hang upside down
by his back toes
from a bird feeder."

"And I can swim too.
I don't love it, like cousin beaver,
but I can hoggy-paddle."

"Well . . . ahh . . . umm . . . if you must bring that up—
okay, we're not all that quick, as animals go.
But we can run as fast as an average fourth-grader."

"Betcha can't sneak up on me!
I'm very alert. That's how I deal with predators.
My head is like a submarine periscope—
my eyes, ears and nose are set up high
so I can see what's around."

"Snoot in the air is right!
And if your head gets any bigger,
you'll never get down your hole."

PREDATORS

FOX

BIRDS OF PREY

DOG

COYOTE

SQUIRREL

"My nose is so terrific that I've got
my own 'Caller ID' system—
if you've been by my burrow for a visit,
I'll know about it."

"He smells, he hears, he sees . . .
he swims and climbs trees . . .
anything else, Mr. Wonderful?"

"Yes, I can live in all kinds of places—
fields, woods, thickets, rocky areas
or under sheds and porches . . .
I'm not fussy."

"Same is true for eating—not picky there either.
I'll eat grass, dandelion greens, clover, grains,
bark, insects, fruits, veggies . . ."

"Speaking of eating, my chompers aren't just for chewing. My fabulous teeth even help dig my burrow. They're strong enough to gnaw through roots and move rocks. And I can chatter my teeth so loudly that my enemies turn and flee. Can you do that? Didn't think so—well, I can do that and more."

"I have special teeth that keep growing. Gnawing keeps them just the right length. Too long, like that beak of yours, wouldn't be good."

"Hey, we squirrels have those kind of teeth too. Maybe we really are related. But how do you keep your teeth short during that long snooze?"

"Hibernating, not snoozing!
It's not the same as snoozing—
there's more to it.
Before the weather gets cold,
we snack like mad and cover
our bodies with fat."

"You mean pig out.
Whistle pig out!"

"Shh. I want to hear
about the teeth."

"I'm getting to that. When I'm ready to hibernate,
I go down into my burrow and seal myself into a lower chamber
so that no one will disturb me. In my hibernation slumber,
I barely breathe . . . only about once every six minutes.
And my heart beats only once every four or five minutes.
Everything slows way down. My teeth even stop growing."

"That's amazing."

"It must be very
dark and stuffy
in there. And don't
you get hungry?"

"Well, yes, but . . . ahem . . . when
the days are warmer, I also feel
the need for a snack and a date
with a mate. When I find a mate I like,
we chuckle and chatter at each other,
and we touch noses and rub cheeks."

"I'm not only cute, I'm helpful.
Scientists are trying to figure out
if people could hibernate, as groundhogs do.
They study us to learn more about
body rhythms and cycles of animals,
including people."

"Maybe one day folks will climb aboard a space vehicle, hibernate, and wake up on Mars!"

"You're the Hog!
Operation Groundhog
will start immediately.
The world will know
the Hog truth."